My Life as a
CHINESE
IMMIGRANT

Gareth Stevens
PUBLISHING

By Max Caswell

Please visit our website, www.garethstevens.com. For a free color catalog of all our high-quality books, call toll free 1-800-542-2595 or fax 1-877-542-2596.

Library of Congress Cataloging-in-Publication Data

Names: Caswell, Max, author.
Title: My life as a Chinese immigrant / Max Caswell.
Description: New York : Gareth Stevens Publishing, [2018] | Series: My place in history | Includes index.
Identifiers: LCCN 2017007386| ISBN 9781538202937 (pbk. book) | ISBN 9781538202944 (6 pack) | ISBN 9781538202951 (library bound book)
Subjects: LCSH: Chinese–United States–History–19th century–Juvenile literature. | Chinese Americans–United States–History–19th century–Juvenile literature. | Central Pacific Railroad Company–History–Juvenile literature. | Pacific railroads–Juvenile literature.
Classification: LCC E184.C5 C26 2018 | DDC 973/.04951–dc23
LC record available at https://lccn.loc.gov/2017007386

Published in 2018 by
Gareth Stevens Publishing
111 East 14th Street, Suite 349
New York, NY 10003

Copyright © 2018 Gareth Stevens Publishing

Designer: Bethany Perl
Editor: Joan Stoltman

Photo credits: Cover, p. 1 courtesy of the Library of Congress; cover, p. 1 (background) Natalia Sheinkin/Shutterstock.com; cover, pp. 1–24 (torn strip) barbaliss/Shutterstock.com; cover, pp. 1–24 (photo frame) Davor Ratkovic/Shutterstock.com; cover, pp. 1–24 (white paper) HABRDA/Shutterstock.com; cover, pp. 1–24 (parchment) M. Unal Ozmen/Shutterstock.com; cover, pp. 1–24 (textured edge) saki80/Shutterstock.com; pp. 1–24 (paper background) Kostenko Maxim/Shutterstock.com; pp. 5 (tea carrier), 17 Bettmann/Getty Images; p. 5 (tea leaves) Shulevskyy Volodymyr/Shutterstock.com; p. 7 Kean Collection/Archive Photos/Getty Images; p. 9 courtesy of US National Archives and Records Administration; p. 11 NNhering/iStockphoto.com; p. 13 Marzolino/Shutterstock.com; p. 15 CORBIS/Corbis Historical/Getty Images; p. 19 (telegram) RedKnight7/Wikipedia.org; p. 19 (inset) Andrew J. Russell/Wikipedia.org; p. 21 (map) Intellson/Shutterstock.com; p. 21 (railroad tracks) Everett Historical/Shutterstock.com.

Printed in the United States of America

CPSIA compliance information: Batch #CS17GS: For further information contact Gareth Stevens, New York, New York at 1-800-542-2595.

CONTENTS

Words in the glossary appear in **bold** type the first time they are used in the text.

Feeding the WORKERS

March 17, 1865

Central Pacific hired Father and me to cook for their Chinese railroad workers. Mother stayed back in Sacramento, California, to run our store. Our store sells everything my parents missed when they first came to California from China—dried vegetables, teas, dried pork, noodles, and dried fish. Now, Father and I don't sell, we cook—day and night!

We speak Chinese at my school and home, but my friend Jian and I practice English whenever we can! This journal is how I'll practice without Jian around.

Notes from History

Built from 1863 to 1869, the transcontinental railroad was built by two rail companies. Their lines would connect and cross much of the country. The Central Pacific Railroad Company built the part that ran from Sacramento to Promontory Summit, Utah.

tea leaves

The Chinese workers drank
tea with boiled water, and ate
foods with lots of vegetables.
This kept them healthier than
the white railroad workers.

5

Our WORK

April 29, 1865

We're camped a few feet away from our cooking tent. Every month, Father sends a **telegram** to Mother with our order of supplies, which she sends from Sacramento the following week. I'm only 9, but I'm the helper cook!

Every day except Sunday the men work 12 hours on the railroad. So, we start cooking before the sun rises and finish after it's gone down. Every few days, we pack up our sleeping and cooking tents and hike to the next campsite.

Notes from History

The Chinese workers were mostly poor, male, teenaged farmers. They were hired in China and brought by boats. The non-Chinese workers were Irish **immigrants**, members of the Mormon Church, and Civil War soldiers.

No one knows how many Chinese workers built the transcontinental railroad.

Some historians guess 10,000 to 12,000, but others say double that!

Not LIKE THEM

October 13, 1865

    All day and night, I **stoke** the fire for the tea and carry buckets of tea to the crew as they shovel, lift, hammer, and build!

    The workers don't know I know English. They **mock** our food, looks, and hats and don't know I understand. They even mock us for bathing and washing our clothes. Yesterday, some of the white men set one of the Chinese sleeping tents on fire! I don't know why they're angry, since they're paid more.

Notes from History

The Central Pacific Railroad went east from Sacramento for 690 miles (1,110 km). It cut through **granite** mountains.

Chinese workers on the transcontinental railroad were paid less than white workers for longer hours. They also paid for food, housing, tools, clothes, and medical care that the white workers got for free!

Life at CAMP

March 4, 1866

The men tell us they "only" lay 2 miles (3.2 km) of track daily. That sounds like a lot to me. I can't imagine them working harder! I'm told there are 600 miles (966 km) to go!

Every day, they use axes and shovels to move trees, roots, and huge rocks out of the way. I've even seen them build bridges. Today, I can see mountains in the distance. Father says the men will have to blast tunnels right through them!

Notes from History

Every morning, a train would back down the already laid track and deliver rails and other supplies for the day's work. Every few days, the workers' campsite was moved around 25 miles (40 km) to the new end of the track.

Every job building the railroad was hard, but some jobs, like placing explosives, were downright dangerous! Chinese workers earned extra pay doing dangerous jobs the white workers wouldn't do.

TUNNEL #6

August 29, 1866

Now that we're in the mountains, the work isn't so much about laying track as it is digging tunnels. I'm told they'll make 15 tunnels using black powder, or gunpowder, to blast through the rock. They were going to use **nitroglycerin**, but no one would work with that deadly stuff!

Our **gang**'s been assigned to the **Summit** Tunnel, or Tunnel #6. They work in three **shifts** around the clock because winter is coming. This means Father and I also work around the clock to feed all the shifts.

Notes from History

A crate carrying nitroglycerin to the railroad exploded in San Francisco, California, killing 15 people and destroying a building! After that, gunpowder was used in its place.

Building tunnels through the Sierra Nevada was mostly done by blasting through the hard granite with explosives. After a blast formed a cave, workers would cart out rocks and rubble, and then place more explosives.

EXPLOSION!

October 20, 1866

    We're up at 2 o'clock in the morning feeding the third shift. The next shift's explosions have started up already. We're used to the sound now.

    Just now, I heard an explosion and then yelling. Father has me stay back, but I already know what's happened because it happened last week, too. Some of the gunpowder failed, but no one knew. The men went into the tunnel to fill their carts, and then it exploded, killing 21 men. I wonder how many have died this time.

Notes from History

No records were kept of Chinese deaths, only white deaths. Historians use sources from the time to find out more about **avalanches**, explosions, falls, and accidents during the building of the transcontinental railroad.

There was no such thing as safety when you worked on the railroad.

Up to 1,200 Chinese workers may have died, but only 137 Chinese deaths were ever written about.

A Terrible WINTER

January 12, 1867

Our gang's on Tunnel #10 now. We're buried in snow. I haven't seen the sun in 2 weeks. The workers have tunneled through the snow to connect their sleeping tents to our cooking tent. They've even dug us a **chimney**! The snow is sometimes 4 stories high, so 30 workers in our gang now do nothing but shovel the tunnel entrance.

The snow blocked the supply train this month, so Father's had to **ration** food. He feels terrible about it but says it must be done.

Notes from History

Despite 44 snowstorms, 11 tunnels were built the winter of 1866 to 1867. Avalanches at Tunnels #11 and #12 swept entire camps of Chinese workers off the side of the mountain to their death.

For 3 months during the winter, no work was possible. Almost 8,000 workers, mostly Chinese, lived under the snow with little food, little warmth, and no pay!

Finally FINISHED

May 10, 1869

I can't believe it's true! For years, I have watched the railroad grow ever eastbound. Today, we're in Promontory Summit, Utah, and it's complete! There are newspaper reporters and railroad bosses everywhere, excitedly awaiting the final **spike**. I heard a story that the spike's connected to telegraph wires so the hammering can be heard instantly in New York City and San Francisco!

It's very strange: none of the speeches are mentioning us at all. It's as if we Chinese don't count!

Notes from History

Several photographs were taken of the workers that day, but there isn't a Chinese face among them. They were in Promontory Summit but may not have been invited to the event.

WESTERN UNION
TELEGRAM
W. P. MARSHALL, PRESIDENT

1201

May 10th, 1869

To: His Excellency, General Ulysses S. Grant, President of the United States Washington, D.C.

SIR: We have the honor to report that the last rail is laid, the last spike is driven. The Pacific Railroad is finished.

From: Leland Stanford, President, Central Pacific Railroad Co. of California

T.P. Durant, Vice-President, Union Pacific Railroad Company

TELEPHONE No. ....

TELEPHONED TO ....

TIME 12:00 pm

BY .... TO BE ....

ATTEMPTS }
TO   }
DELIVER }

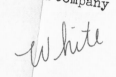

White House

THE COMPAN... ...ATRONS CONCERNING ITS SERVICE

A telegram saying this was sent to President Grant during the big event!

19

What Will They DO NOW?

June 25, 1869

Part of the railroad back near Sacramento needed fixing, so we headed there with our gang after Promontory Summit. Today, we celebrate the real end of the work! Father's been saving all four of our chickens and a pig for this meal. The men are very pleased!

They say there's much more fixing to be done and more railroads to build, but we're headed back home. I wonder what'll happen to these men. Maybe Father can help some of them find work!

Notes from History

Few Chinese workers could afford to return home to China or bring their families. Most stayed in the United States, often hired by other Chinese to work at farms, mines, laundries, cafes, and restaurants.

TRANSCONTINENTAL RAILROAD

Oregon

Montana

North Dakota

Minnesota

Idaho

PROMONTORY SUMMIT

South Dakota

Wyoming

Nevada

Iowa

Nebraska

OMAHA

SACRAMENTO

Utah

California

Colorado

Kansas

Arizona

New Mexico

- Central Pacific line
- Union Pacific line

The Union Pacific Railroad Company built the other half of the transcontinental railroad.

GLOSSARY

avalanche: a large mass of snow sliding down a mountain

chimney: a part of a building through which smoke rises to the outside

gang: in railroad work, the group of men who work together

granite: a rough, very hard rock

immigrant: one who comes to a country to settle there

mock: to make fun of someone by copying a way of behaving or speaking

nitroglycerin: a highly explosive, dangerous liquid that is man-made

ration: to control the amount of food that people have when the supply is limited

shift: a group of people who work together during a specific period of time

spike: a large nail used to attach rails to railroad ties made of wood

stoke: to stir or add fuel to something that is burning

summit: the top of a mountain

telegram: a message sent by telegraph, which uses electric signals sent through wires

For more INFORMATION

Books

Bailer, Darice. *The Last Rail: The Building of the First Transcontinental Railroad.* Norwalk, CT: Soundprints, 2011.

Kuskowski, Alex. *Cool Pacific Coast Cooking: Easy and Fun Regional Recipes.* Minneapolis, MN: ABDO Publishing Company, 2014.

Wilson, Steve. *The California Gold Rush: Chinese Laborers in America (1848–1882).* New York, NY: PowerKids Press, 2016.

Websites

Building the Transcontinental Railroad
pbs.org/wgbh/americanexperience/features/photo-gallery/tcrr-gallery/
Browse photographs of the building of the transcontinental railroad.

The Race to Utah!
pbs.org/wgbh/americanexperience/features/flash-interactive/tcrr/
Read and see the railroad's progress on this clickable map.

INDEX